How I Made Money

During

The Great Market Crash of 2008

Illustrated with Actual Trading Records

A Stock Market Investment Strategy

Jamin Chen

Title: How I Made Money during the Great Market Crash of 2008

Published by CCO Inc, Montville, NJ 07045

Library of Congress Control Number: 2009903692

ISBN: 978-0-578-02070-9

Printed in the United States of America.

May 2009.

A Word from the Author

I am not a financial advisor. I have not had financial training. I am just one who did some research on this topic and came up with the investment strategy described here. I am here to describe to you my experience and my view of making money in the stock market. I am not suggesting that you, the reader, to follow this strategy. Every strategy has its own time and place. This strategy is no exception. I did make money with this strategy during the great market crash of 2008. Just before the publication of this book, the market had been dropping downward toward a Dow Jones Industrial Average of 6,000. A strategy similar to the one described in this book had been applied. However, how this strategy will pan out in this environment would not be known for some time, since this was only the first leg of the downward movement of the market. Nevertheless, I would like to share with you my experience of the last three months of 2008. The strategy described here had worked for me during that period; however, it may not work under different sets of circumstances. You may adopt this strategy only by your own choice. Before you do anything with this strategy, you must study this strategy carefully yourself and understand how it worked and why it worked. Always consult with your own financial advisor and get his or her opinion before you do anything suggested in this book.

Acknowledgements

My greatest appreciation goes to Ivy Kaminsky who provided the major editing of this book. My thanks also go to my friends, Benjamin Weng and Ann Yuan, who had been my sounding boards as I developed my strategy, as well as Alfred Chau and Warren Leung, who also helped me in completing this book. I also like to express my gratitude to my son-in-law Dik Blewitt for the encouragement he had given me in publishing this book.

Table of Contents

Chapter 1

Introduction

This book is about investing in the stock market. More specifically, it is about investing *only* in a particular ETF (Exchange Traded Fund) called DIA, or Diamonds, which tracks the performance of the Dow Jones Industrial Average, DJIA.

There are many reasons for choosing DIA. Among them are its safety and predictability.

This book describes a strategy with which you can make steady profit from trading in DIA without taking too great a risk. The strategy is a conservative one. You will not make a "killing" in the market with it. This book is not for people who are looking for a get-rich-quick scheme.

If you are inclined to invest in individual stocks, with the intention of making more money per trade, this book is not for you.

This strategy does not use options nor does it rely on buying stocks on margin. These are very risky strategies and they pose a real possibility of losing all you have. The strategy described here is based on holding the long position at all times, i.e., you own the stocks you buy free and clear.

The strategy is rather conservative and you make only a small amount of money on each trade. The strategy depends heavily on frequent trading. It is not a "buy and hold" strategy. It requires great discipline to follow this strategy. However, if you are patient and disciplined, you may be rewarded with profits which few mutual funds can provide.

The strategy has been in development for the last six years and it reached its present form at the onset of the great market crash of 2008. I made money with it even during that dark period when many investors were scared by the plummeting values of their portfolios.

This book is written for people who have at least $100,000 to invest in the stock market. You may start with $50,000 but it will be somewhat more difficult to make money with that amount.

If you have $250,000 or more to invest, you will feel a lot more comfortable and secure with this strategy.

The capital requirement described above is probably applicable to most investments in the stock market based on long positions.

The dollar amount of each trade in the strategy described in this book is from $5,000 to $10,000, and the strategy attempts to profit only about $200 from each trade. Therefore, with about $100,000 to invest, you can hold about 10 trades or positions on your book simultaneously.

The trading cost is about $10 to $15 per trade. So, if you trade at much less than $10,000 per trade for a long position, it is really hard to make money. For example, for a trade of $1,000, the transaction cost of $10 is around 1% of the trading value. A round trip (one buy and one sell) would cost you $20 or about 2%. The strategy described in this book aims to make only about 2% per round trip, therefore it does not work with trading at the $1,000 level. If you trade at the $1,000 level with this strategy, you would essentially wind up working for the brokerage company handling your account.

You must realize that there is no such thing as a "fool-proof" strategy, especially when making money in the stock market. This book does not make any guarantee nor imply that you will make money with the strategy described in this book. However, if you judiciously adapt this strategy, there is a good chance you will make money.

In the following,

Chapter 2 gives the essence of the strategy.

Chapter 3 describes some variations of the strategy.

Chapter 4 gives an example of actual application of this strategy.

Chapter 5 presents the market data that support the strategy.

The remaining chapters provide some more supporting materials to this strategy.

Chapter 2

The Essence of the Strategy

In essence, you establish your investment strategy based on the long term behavior of the stock market. No single investment strategy will let you make money all the time. Each strategy works only under certain circumstances. The strategy described here is no exception.

We are now in a period when the Dow Jones Industrial Average (DJIA) is lingering below its historical trend line. I will explain in more detail later what I mean by "historical trend line." For the next few years (starting at the present, i.e., the year 2009 and a few years hereafter) this trend line is likely to remain between 8,000 and 10,000.

The DJIA is calculated based on the performance of 30 select companies. For the last 80 years (i.e., the entire history of the DJIA), the DJIA has been rising at an average rate of more than 6% a year. However, this was not a straight progression. Instead, the DJIA deviated widely from its historical trend: at its highest it was as high as 100% above the trend line; at its lowest it was as much as 50% below it. Stated otherwise, in extreme cases, the DJIA may go as high as 20,000 and as low as 5,000 over the next few years. Such extremes appear unlikely but they could happen. Lately, we have seen it reach 14,000, at its highest, and now it is heading toward 6,000.

The strategy outlined in this book is for when the DJIA is below 10,000 and assumes it might even go down as low as 5,000 in some unlucky set of circumstances.

This strategy is based on trading the ETF called DIA which tracks the performance of the DJIA. The value of each share of DIA is about $1/100^{th}$ of the DJIA. Therefore, this strategy is for trading DIA when its value is between $50 and $100 per share.

The strategy is essentially as follows:

> In a falling market, the strategy would be to *buy* 100 shares of DIA when its value drops every $2 below $100 (or when the DJIA drops every 200 points below 10,000).

> In a rising market, the strategy would be to *sell* 100 shares of DIA when its value rises $2 above the last purchase price of DIA.

Suppose you start this strategy when DIA is $100. You start buying lots of 100 shares of DIA at $98 and then $96 and downward until it turns around and starts going up.

Suppose the market goes down and DIA hits $91 before it starts to turn around. By this time, you will have accumulated 400 shares of DIA, having bought at $98, $96, $94, and $92, respectively.

When the market turns around and starts going up, you sell the DIA you bought at $2 above your purchase price. In other words, you sell the $92 lot at $94, the $94 lot at $96, the $96 lot at $98, and the $98 lot at $100.

Thus, you will have made $200 for each round trip (or a pair of trades).

In this example, for simplicity, all commissions are ignored. The effects of commissions will be dealt with later.

That is all there is to this strategy.

Simple, isn't it?

Let me summarize the four basic parts of this strategy:

1. **Trading Range** – This strategy is applicable only for DIA between $50 and $100. This range is called the trding range.

2. **Trading Lot** –The shares bought in each trade is called the trading lot and the

number of shares bought in each lot is called the lot size or the trading size and it is 100 shares. Each lot of DIA is also called one position.

3. **Trading Interval** – One lot or 100 shares of DIA is bought with each drop of $2 in the price of DIA. This $2 interval is called the trading interval.

4. **Markup** – Each lot of DIA is sold at $2 above the price at which it was bought. This $2 differential between the buy price and the sell price is called the markup. In this strategy, both the trading interval and the markup happen to be $2. It is just a coincidence.

There are several things you should be aware of and there are also some variations to this strategy. I will describe them below.

2.1   When the DJIA is Below 10,000

Use this strategy only when the DJIA is below 10,000. The reason is that for now and the next few years, a DJIA above 10,000 may mean the market is over-valued (more on this later). The market tends to correct itself and, therefore, when it is over-valued, it will most probably correct itself by going down. However, we do not know when this correction will take place. It may happen in the next few days or in the next few years. When it happens, the DJIA may drop so fast that you cannot get rid of your positions in time. Witness how fast the market went down in the great market crash of 2008: from September to November, it went from about 12,000 to below 8,000, just three short months. And, it again dropped from about 9,000 to below 7,000 in the first two months of 2009.

Thus, if you had held DIA bought at $130 or so, you would have incurred a great loss using this strategy.

On the other hand, when the DJIA is below 10,000, it is generally under-valued. It appears that the DJIA may stay below 10,000 for the time being and the next few years. During this period, if DJIA does drop significantly below 10,000, it may correct itself and eventually go back up toward 10,000. The strategy outlined in this book is based on this assumption and it is applicable only when the DJIA is below 10,000. In other words, a DJIA of 10,000 or its DIA equivalent of

$100 is the upper limit of the trading range of this strategy.

2.2 How Great is Your Possible Exposure?

In 2009, the DJIA started the year by hovering below 10,000. Its past performance shows that, on several occasions, the DJIA has gone down by as much as 50% from its historical trend. Therefore, it is reasonable to assume that it could again go down as much during the current financial crises to as low as 5,000, or the DIA equivalent of $50.

Therefore, a DJIA of 5,000 or its DIA equivalent of $50 is the lower limit of the trading range of this strategy.

In the hypothetical case that the DJIA goes all the way down to 5,000 and DIA reaches $50, and you had been buying 100 shares of DIA for every $2 drop, and you had started buying at $98,

- you would have bought a total of 25 lots and have in your possession 2,500 shares of DIA

- at a total cost of $185,000 plus commissions, and

- an average cost of $74 per share, plus commissions.

Therefore, if you had reserved about $200,000 for this strategy, you could weather a severe market downturn all the way down to a DJIA of 5,000.

What happens if the market does go all the way down to a DJIA of 5,000? It could be a temporary dip in the market. It could signal a significant change in the market behavior. It is difficult and impossible to gauge its significance before it happens.

When it does happen, you may

1. Liquidate your position.

2. Keep buying for every $2 drop, or

3. Stop buying DIA when it hits $50,

It is your choice and therein lies the risk of this strategy.

In any case, a DJIA of 5,000 or its DIA equivalent of $50 is the lower limit of the trading range of this strategy.

2.2.1 Liquidate Your Position

If you liquidate your position, you will recover approximately $125,000 with a loss of about $60,000, not counting expenses like commissions. You may look at this $60,000 as the most you will lose with this strategy.

If you cannot afford this loss, do not follow this strategy.

Please note that if the DJIA could go from above 14,000 to below 8,000 in 2008 and drop further to below 7,000 in 2009, it could go down to 5,000 any time.

Therefore, if you ignore the possibility of the DJIA going below 5,000 in the next few years, do so at your own peril.

2.2.2 Keep Investing

Of course you can keep buying DIA for every $2 drop even as it falls below $50. In other words, you will be expanding your lower limit of your tranding range.

The worst case scenario is if the DJIA were to go to zero, then DIA would be 0. That would mean all corporations in the United States would cease to exist. That is entirely impossible, though the DJIA could theoretically approach zero in a financial calamity.

So, if you buy DIA from $48 all the way down to $2, you would have bought another 24 lots and increased your holding by another 2,400 shares with an additional outlay of $60,000.

By then you would have put out a total of $245,000, including those shares of DIA you bought when it was above $50.

So, if the economy of the United States tanks, the total exposure you will have with this strategy is about $250,000.

You may think this is an unlikely scenario. However, at the least, you ought to take a look at this possibility to know what your maximum exposure could be.

On the other hand, if you intend to follow this strategy all the way to a DJIA of zero, you may set aside $250,000 for it. For you to follow this strategy to this extent, you would have to have a lot of faith in the vitality of the United States that the DJIA would eventually recover to 10,000 and above, even after a financial catastroph of such scale.

However, when you are about to continue following this strategy below a DIA of $50, you should seriously consider whether you are recklessly following it, risking everything you have invested already, plus the additional fund you are going to invest in it.

2.2.3 Stop Buying

If your threshold of pain is not high and the DJIA is going down and approaching 5,000, and you cannot stomach any more downward movemnet but you don't want to liquidate your position, then just stop buying any more.

If history is any guide, the DJIA will eventually go back up to 10,000. It is just that nobody knows for sure how long it will take for this to happen. It could be a few months, or a few decades.

One advantage of this strategy is that you hold the long position at all times. This means you can afford to wait for the market to recover. Unlike holding short positions, there is no time pressure to liquidate your position. Stock prices rise with inflation. Part of the rise in the DJIA can be traced to inflation and another part to the increase in productivity. Inflation and productivity increases are two major driving forces behind the ever rising DJIA. Therefore, the DJIA will certainly get over 10,000 again someday, although it may take decades

In the unlikely event that the market does not recover in your lifetime, you can always will your shares to your offspring.

Chapter 3

Variations in Strategy

In the previous chapter, I illustrate the basic form of the strategy. There are many variations to it. The following is a description of some of them.

3.1 Getting Started

When you are getting started, DIA may be over $100 a share. In that case, you should wait until it goes below $100 to start using this strategy. Ideally you should wait until it is below $90.

On the other hand, if DIA is lower than $90, say, $86, when you are about to start, you may start by buying 100 shares of DIA at $86. In that case, if DIA goes up to $88, you will have sold out all of your position and you will have nothing to sell if DIA keeps going up. So, one possible strategy to use is to make an initial buy of 700 shares so that you can sell 100 shares for every $2 rise in DIA until it hits $100. Whether you buy 100 shares, 700 shares, or any number of shares in between, it depends on your outlook on the market and it is your decision.

If you think the DIA will not go above $90 any time soon and you do not want to tie up your money now, you may buy only 200 shares for possible sells at $88 and $90. In doing so, you are setting $90 as the upper limit of your trading range.

3.2   Strike Price

You do not have to buy or sell DIA at an exact dollar price, for example, buying at $82.00 and selling at $84.00. You may set all your trades at any price, say, buy at $82.23 and sell at $84.23, as long as you set the difference between the buy and sell prices or the markup at $2.00.

Even this $2.00 difference or markup is not sacrosanct. You may set it at $2.20 to cover the trading cost or commission so that you would net about $200 for each round trip (or a pair of trades). For example, you may buy at $82.00 and sell at $84.20.

The markup of about $2 is set primarily to make sufficient amount of money per trade while covering your trading cost. Most brokerage commissions are about $10 per trade. A round trip of trades should cost about $20. So, if you make about $200 per round trip, the trading cost is about 10%. Therefore, it is up to you to decide whether you want to make about $180 or $200 per round trip and set your markup accordingly.

There may be some advantages to trading at a few cents below or above the round dollar values. Round figures are easy to work with and many people like to trade using round figures. As a result, some people may take advantage of it and trade at a few cents below or above the round dollar to stay ahead of their fellow traders.

3.3 If You Want to Risk Less

If you want to risk less money using this strategy, there are several ways to do it.

However I would not recommend working with less than 100 shares per trade. It is because, if you use a smaller number of shares per trade, your trading costs will eat up a larger portion of the potential profit from this strategy and you may end up working for the brokerage house.

3.3.1 Same Trading Intervals

You can choose to follow this strategy as laid out above. You are supposed to keep buying DIA for every $2 drop until DIA hits $50. However, you are free to set a different lower limit for when to call it quit.

For example, instead of waiting for DIA to hit $50 before deciding to either stop trading or to liquidate your position, you may set your lower limit at $60, $70, or even $80. This is entirely up to you.

In other words, you may lower the amount of money at risk by working with a narrower trading range that has a higher lower limit.

Or, you may lower your upper limit by starting this strategy when DIA is below $90 or even lower, instead of $100 as suggested above.

3.3.2 Larger Trading Intervals

You may opt to buy DIA at every $3 drop instead of every $2 drop as described above and sell it every time it goes up $3.

Your exposure when DIA gets down to $50, if it ever does, would be only two-thirds as much as it would be if your trading interval is $2. However, a swing of $3 in DIA, equivalent to a 300 point swing in DJIA, will occur less frequently than $2 swing. Consequently, you will trade less often and make less money in proportion to the amount of capital you put to invest.

3.4   If You Want to Take on More Risk

If you would like to put more money into this strategy, there are several ways to do it. You may

1. Decrease the size of trading intervals,

2. Increase the size of each trade, or

3. Decrease the markup while increasing the size of each trade.

These variations are discussed below.

3.4.1 Decrease the Trading Intervals

In this variation, instead of buying 100 shares of DIA with each $2 drop in its price, you may buy them with each $1 drop, for example, at $84, $83, $82, and on down. When you do so, you have doubled your investment in this strategy. Of course, for each 100 shares of DIA you bought, you would sell them again at $2 above the buy price or with a markup of $2. This means you would only sell the 100 shares you bought at $82 at $84 or higher.

With this halving of trading intervals, you will probably trade more than twice as often and make more than twice the money you would have made if you had been trading at the $2 interval. This is because sometimes DIA may swing more than $2 but not between the two even dollar prices of DIA. In other words, DIA may swing between $83 and $85 and had you bought at $83, you would then be able to make a $2 profit when it rose to $85. On the other hand, if you had waited to buy at $82 and it never gets there, you would not be able to make either the $83-$85 trade or the $82-$84 trade.

If you want to invest four times as often as the basic strategy, you may decrease the trading intervals to $0.50 or 50 cents. Now, you buy 100 shares of DIA for each 50 cent drop in its price. Still, you would want to sell each lot of 100 shares you bought at $2 or more above the buy price.

Then if you want to invest eight times as often, you may decrease the trading interval to $0.25 or 25 cents.

3.4.2 Increase the Trading Size

With any trading interval suggested in the preceding section, you can also increase your investment by merely making the size of each trade larger. You may buy and sell 200 shares each time instead of 100 shares. Or, 300 shares, or 400 shares, or any size you like.

3.4.3 Decrease the Markup with Increased Trading Size

When you increase the trading size, say, to 200 shares for each pair of buys and sells, you can now afford to sell the shares at only $1 markup above the buy price while keeping the trading cost (commissions) below 10% of the profit.

If you trade in 400 share lots, you may work with a markup of only $0.50 while again keeping the trading cost below 10% of the profit.

With this variation, you will again be trading more frequently and you may make more money than directly proportional to the money you put at risk. However, you should be fully aware that you are putting more money at risk and if something unforeseen happens, you stand to lose more.

3.5   Buying for the Future

When the DJIA drops down to, say, 8,000 or below, you may start to think about whether or not you should "buy and hold" some DIA for when the DJIA returns to 10,000 or even to its previous high of 13,000 in some distant future.

For example, if you buy 100 shares of DIA at $80 and you hold it until it rises to, say, $130, you would make $50 on an $80 investment.

If the DJIA returns to 13,000 in two years, you would make about 30% per year on your investment.

If it takes three years, then your return would be about 20% per year.

If it takes four years, the return would be less than 15% per year compounded over four years.

If it takes five years, the return would be less then 10% per year compounded.

You can also look at such purchases for the future in a different way, as follows.

Suppose you buy 1,500 shares of DIA at a price below $100 before the DJIA makes its recovery and rises above 10,000. Now, you can sell them off 100 shares at a time for each $2 interval above $100. And after each time you sell 100 shares, you can buy them back when their price drops $2 below the sell price.

This is the reverse of the basic strategy described above.

With 1,500 shares, you will not exhaust your inventory of DIA until the DJIA hits 13,000 using this reverse strategy.

This is something you can keep in mind.

Chapter 4

Actual Trading Example

Here I am going to show you how I actually traded during the great market crash of 2008. I will also talk about several important things you need to know about trading with this strategy.

4.1   The Trading Record

I started following this particular strategy outlined above on October 7th and by October 31st, the market made some dramatic gyrations and DIA had visited below $80 during that time period.

The maximum capital layout I had during that period was $89,000. Since the market does not go straight down or straight up, it made several reversals in this period and I made quite a few trades resulting in a realized gain of $4,145. The actual gain is somewhat less than this because it does not take into account the trading commissions.

In less than a month, I made 4.7% on my invested capital. It is too early to say how long this good return would continue. However, if they can be maintained for the entire year to come, I may make a better than 50% return per year on my invested capital.

The following is a detailed account of the trades I made during this period.

Target	Buy Date	Price	Sell Date	Price	Net
98	10/7/2008	98.00			
96	10/7/2008	96.00			
94	10/8/2008	93.70			
92	10/8/2008	92.00	10/31/2008	94.00	200.00

90	10/11/2008	87.17	10/17/2008	92.00	483.00
	10/17/2008	90.00	10/20/2008	92.00	200.00
	10/21/2008	90.00	10/29/2008	92.00	200.00
	10/29/2008	90.00	10/30/2008	92.00	200.00
	10/30/2008	90.00	10/30/2008	92.00	200.00
88	10/17/2008	88.00	10/20/2008	90.00	200.00
	10/9/2008	86.91	10/17/2008	90.00	309.00
	10/22/2008	88.00	10/28/2008	90.00	200.00
86	10/9/2008	85.60	10/28/2008	88.00	240.00
	10/22/2008	86.00	10/28/2008	89.00	300.00
84	10/16/2008	84.00	10/28/2008	86.00	200.00
	10/22/2008	84.00	10/23/2008	86.00	200.00
82	10/27/2008	81.77	10/27/2008	84.00	223.00
	10/27/2008	82.00	10/28/2008	84.00	200.00
	10/28/2008	82.00	10/28/2008	84.30	230.00
80	10/10/2008	80.00	10/28/2008	83.60	360.00
Total	Buys:	175,515.00	Sells:	150,890.00	4,145.00
Realized net		4,145.00	4.7%		

Max. investment		89,000.00		

Note that on a few occasions, the buys and sells are not at the round dollar amounts the strategy calls for. This is because, in most of these cases, there were dramatic price changes overnight and, in the following morning, I was able to buy them at prices substantially lower than what the strategy called for or sell them at prices substantially higher than what the strategy called for.

It should also be noted that even though there was a net gain at the end of October, depending on the price of DIA, the market value of the DIA I owned could be below or above the total invested capital.

By December 13, about two months after I started this strategy, DIA stood at $86.74 and I had the following results:

Total invested capital	$93,452.75	
Number of shares of DIA owned	1,200	Cost per share $77.88
Price of DIA		$86.74
Market value of investment	$104,088.00	111.4% of total invested capital
Realized gain*	$16,327.25	17.5%

Paper gain**	$10,327.25	11.4%

*Sum of the gains from the paired buys and sells.

**Market value of investments over the total invested capital.

All figures above do not include commissions and other costs associated with the trading.

At this time, I am ahead of the game as long as DIA stays above $77.88.

I must remind you that the performance described above may never happen again. The market is full of surprises, uncertainty, and unpredictability. Whatever you do, you are taking a risk. Therefore, it is important to minimize your risk when you are investing.

In order to reduce the risk of the strategy I am presenting here, I have done some homework. I will describe the homework I did in detail later on in this book.

4.2 The Order Book

On October 31, 2008, the market closed with DIA at $93.15 and a high for the day of $94.53. That day, I sold at $94 the 100 shares of DIA that I had bought at $92. At that moment, my order book looked as follows. All orders are "good till cancel," or GTC (more on GTC in section 4.3 below).

Action	Quantity	Strike Price
Sell	100	100
Sell	100	98
Sell	100	96
Buy	100	92
Buy	100	90
Buy	100	88
Buy	100	86
Buy	100	84
And on down		

Notice that there is a $4 gap between the sell and buy orders. This is the direct result of the $2 trading interval. If both the trading interval and the markup are $1, this gap would be $2.

4.2.1 Alternate Order Books

If you don't trade at round dollars, your order book may look like this:

Action	Quantity	Price
Sell	100	100.03
Sell	100	98.03
Sell	100	96.03
Buy	100	92.03
Buy	100	90.03
Buy	100	88.03
And on down		

Or, if you want to recover your trading cost, your order book might look like this:

Action	Quantity	Price
Sell	100	100.20
Sell	100	98.20
Sell	100	96.20
Buy	100	92
Buy	100	90
Buy	100	88
And on down		

4.3   Disciplines

The most important thing to remember in following this strategy is to stick to it. You must have discipline. When it calls for buy, you buy. When it calls for sell, you sell.

Quite often, when the market is on the rise, you feel like the market will go over the sell price the strategy has set for it and will keep going higher. You feel like you may make more money by waiting a little while longer. However, the market has a way of making unexpected turns. If you don't make the planned sell, the market might just turn around and go down and you would miss your sell opportunity. This situation is often described as "greed" in market parlance.

The reverse is also true. In a down market, you may feel like waiting for the market to go down further than your planned buy price to make your buy. It may just turn around and go up and you would miss your buy opportunity. This situation is often described as "fear" in market parlance.

This strategy depends on making those $2 profits at every chance the market allows. Therefore, it is important to set up an order book as shown previously and stick to it. Perform the trades as planned. The use of Good till Cancel order is one way to adhere to the strategy. A Good till Cancel order is an order to buy or sell a security which remains in effect until executed or canceled.

Fear and greed drive the market. They also blind investors and cause them to lose money in the market.

Following this strategy mechanically will eliminate both fear and greed, that is, the emotional factors in trading. Follow the trading methods outlined here and decide ahead of time how much risk you want to take. Be prepared to stop trading or liquidate your position when the market reaches a certain level. The latter decision is of utmost importance to help you avoid incurring losses that are more than you planned for.

Chapter 5

The Research behind the Strategy

The following is the homework I did as I developed this strategy. This material may be dry and boring; however, you should go over it carefully to determine for yourself if this strategy makes sense to you and to convince yourself of the soundness of its fundamentals. You need to decide for yourself if this strategy can make money for you, and how safe you would feel if you follow this strategy.

You must convince yourself first before you follow this strategy.

5.1 The DJIA Historical Trend Line

The chart below is the monthly performance of the DJIA from late 1928 to January 2009.

Variations in Dow Jones Industiral Average

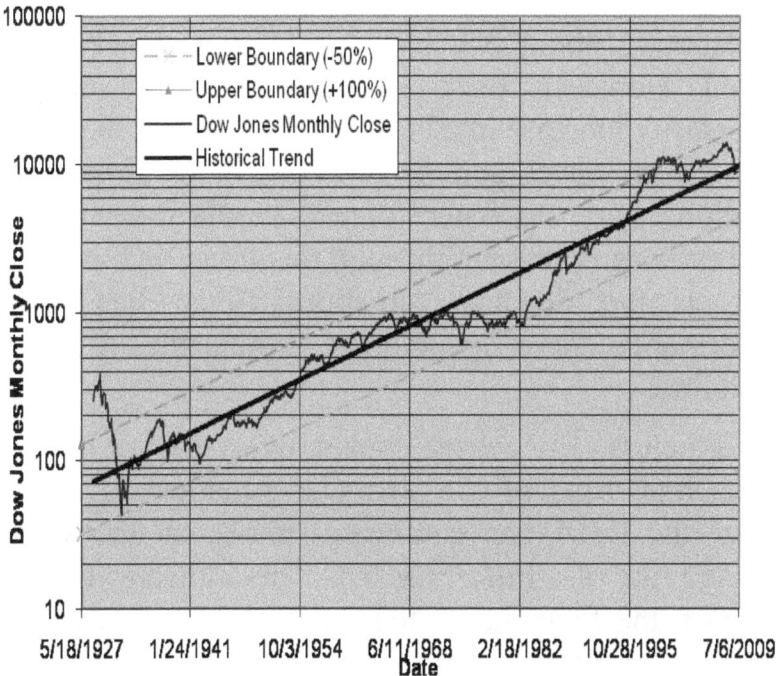

As you can see above you can draw a straight line through the data. This is the solid black line in the middle and I refer to it as the "historical trend line" of the DJIA in this book. The value at any point on this line is called "the historical trend value." This trend line covers more than 80 years of the performance of the DJIA. If history repeats itself, and there is no guarantee that it will, the future performance of the DJIA would appear to follow an extension of this line, that is, continue to keep going up.

This trend line indicates that the DJIA has been rising at an average annual rate of a little over 6%. The two major driving forces behind this steady rise are inflation and increase in productivity, each contributing about 3% each year, over this 80-year period. However, these two driving forces do not necessarily increase at a constant rate. Sometimes they may go up faster and some other times slower. In addition, there are other forces shaping the way the performance is snaking through this trend line. Among them is the financial situation, which bends the performance curve up or down around the historical trend line.

Nevertheless, this chart shows that, even with the twists and turns of the financial situations over the years, the DJIA has continued to rise at an overall average rate of a little over 6%. This indicates that, in the past, the financial system in the United States had corrected itself, and is in essence insulated from all types of intervention, including that of the government. In other words, the DJIA has so far followed this historical trend line, and this could very well be the case, at least in the not so distant future.

In the coming years following the 2008 market crash which is continuing into 2009, there will be a significant business contraction in the United States as well as around the world. This expected contraction will have definite negative effects on the DJIA in the coming years. Whether the massive layoffs occurring now will cause a gain or a loss in productivity is unknown at this time. However, the unprecedented mass injection of money into the financial system by the government will definitely cause inflation in the years to come and this inflation will eventually show up in the DJIA as a gain. With more money chasing more or less the same amount of materials and services, prices will have to go up and so will the profit margins, in terms of absolute dollars, of the companies in the DJIA who provide those materials and services.

Therefore, it is quite possible that the DJIA will resume its climb along the historical trend line once the current financial ills are cured or subside.

The historical data of the DJIA indicates that it will generally continue to rise, even though it may take a long time, maybe decades, from the present downturn. Nevertheless, an investment in DIA today, at below the historical trend line, should have a good chance of providing positive rewards someday.

5.2 Uneven Performance of the DJIA

In the figure above, a dotted line is drawn at 100% above the historical trend line and another dotted line at 50% below the historical trend line. You can see that most of the DJIA performance falls within these two lines, with the exception of the market crash of the late 1920's.

It is legitimate to ask, then, could the current market crash bring the DJIA below the 50% dotted line? It could happen.

After studying the history of the DJIA on the chart above, you could make the following observations:

1. During the tech boom of the late 1990's, the DJIA was more than 100% above the historical trend line. This rise was followed by a fall back down to the historical trend line.

2. In 2007 and 2008, the culmination of easy money policy and subprime mortgages, pushed the DJIA high above the historical trend line, although percentage-wise, it did not go as high as it did during the tech boom of the 90's. Still this rise caused a big drop in late 2008 and now it is below the historical trend. How low it may go below the historical trend line, is anybody's guess.

3. Looking back, following the double booms in the DJIA before and after the 1930 crash, the DJIA did not emerge above the historical trend line for more than 20 years, or until about 1954.

   However, if you had invested soon after the 1929 crash, you would have had an average steady return of 6~7% a year for the next 30 years.

   The growh during this period is about the same as the overall growth rate of the hisorical trend line of the last 8 decades.

4. Once the DJIA crossed over onto the high side of the historical trend line in 1954, it stayed up there and kept rising for about a decade.

5. Then, the DJIA stayed between 600 and 1,000 for the next twenty years, or until 1982.

   Thus, if you had started your investment in 1962, you probabaly would not have seen any gains for the next 20 years.

6. After 1982 the DJIA made a long steady ascent to around 14,000 in the next 18 years, ending with the tech bust of the late 1990's.

   If you were lucky to start investing at around 1982, your investment would have had an average growth of about 13% a year for the next 18 years or so. This growth rate is twice the overall average over the past 80 years.

But, if you had not sold out your position at the peak of the market, your investment would now be heading toward the long term average (the historical trend line) of 9,000 or even lower.

The period of 1980~2000 is a golden period of the market.

You would have had the good fortune to enjoy this golden period only if you had started investing in early 1980's and cashed in all your investment at the peak in 2000.

Many people, including some brokers, like to use this period to say an investment in the stock market can grow at a double digit rate or more than 10% a year.

Yes, it did.

But, the market cannot sustain that kind of growth forever. The big push up of the market in the middle of the first decade of the 21st century ended up in a big thud and the DJIA is now moving toward below 7,000 at the start of 2009.

You may infer from the doldrums that existed during the periods covering the 1940's and 1950's and again during the decade of the 1970's that today the DJIA may have entered into another prolonged doldrum, starting from the end of the tech bust (of the late 1990's) to the beginning of the 21st century. This time, the DJIA may hover around the 8,000-10,000 range for the first two decades of the 21st century.

The strategy presented in this book relies on several assumptions you can see from this chart. They are as follows:

1. According to this chart, the historical trend value of the DJIA should remain between 8,000 and 10,000 for now and for the next few years.

2. The DJIA may hover around 8,000-10,000 for the next few years, and it may go down to 5,000 or up to 20,000 depending on what happens next.

3. If the DJIA dips below the 8,000-10,000 range in the next few years, the chances are good that it will return to the 8,000-10,000 range.

4. If the DJIA rises above the 8,000-10,000 range in the next few years, the chances are good that it will return to the 8,000-10,000 range. Either way, the DJIA should return to this number: 8000-10,000.

5.3   A Summary of DJIA Past Performance

In summary, the past performance of DJIA shows us the following:

- Overall, the DJIA has grown at an average rate of 6~7% a year.

- Sometimes it grew at a rate as high as twice the average rate.

- Other times it did not grow at all.

- Sometimes the DJIA was as high as two times the historical trend line.

- Other times the DJIA was as low as one-half of the historical trend line.

These are important historical facts.

They represent both the predictability and the uncertainty of the performance of the market and hence that of the DJIA.

However, if the past holds true for the future, these facts provide some way of guessing at the future performance of the market. Therefore, we can conclude that the market, and hence the DJIA, may stay around 8,000-10,000 for the first two decades of the 21st century.

We should remember these past performances whenever we are making an investment decision.

5.4   DIA Daily Fluctuations

The DJIA does not stay in one place for long. It fluctuates a lot and provides a lot of opportunities for frequent trading. Here is the difference between the daily highs and lows of the DJIA for 2008 and the first part of 2009.

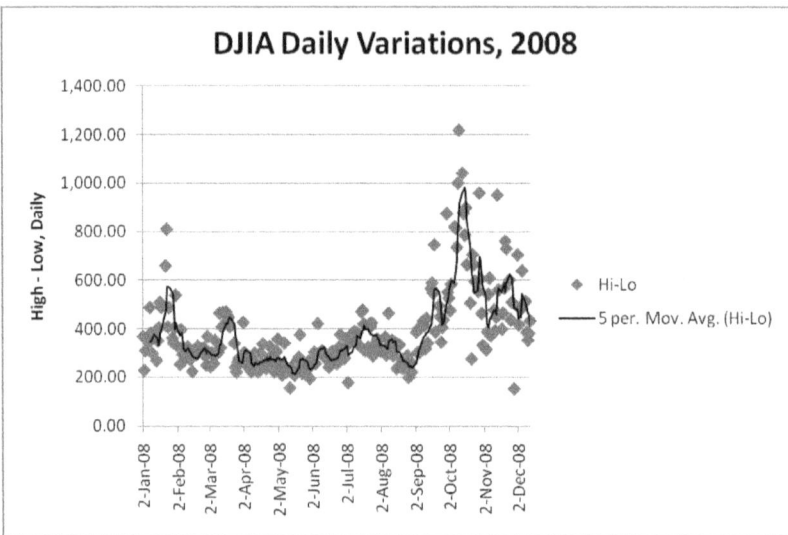

As you can see, the DJIA goes up and down more than 200 points almost every day.

The daily variations of DIA corresponding to the same period are shown below.

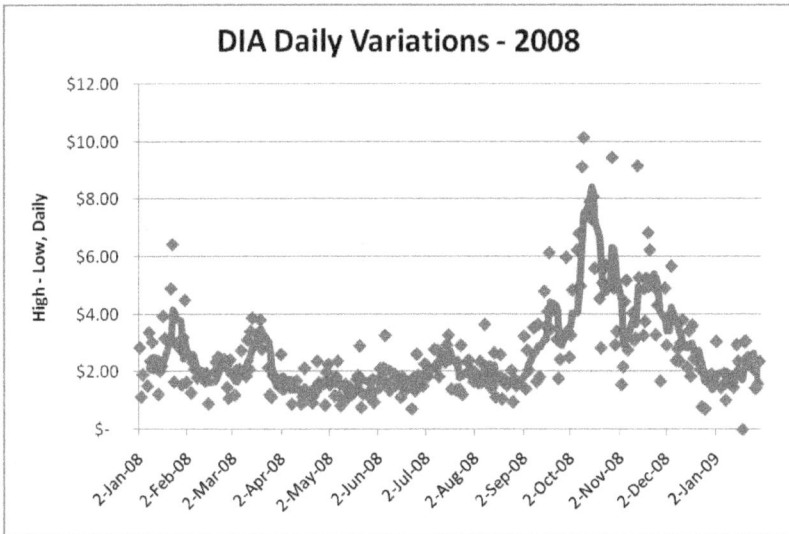

DIA Daily Variations - 2008

Note that DIA fluctuates a little less than the DJIA which it tracks. You may not be able to make a trade every day according to this chart if you trade for a difference of $2.

The following chart shows the weekly variations of DIA:

DIA Weekly Variations - 2008

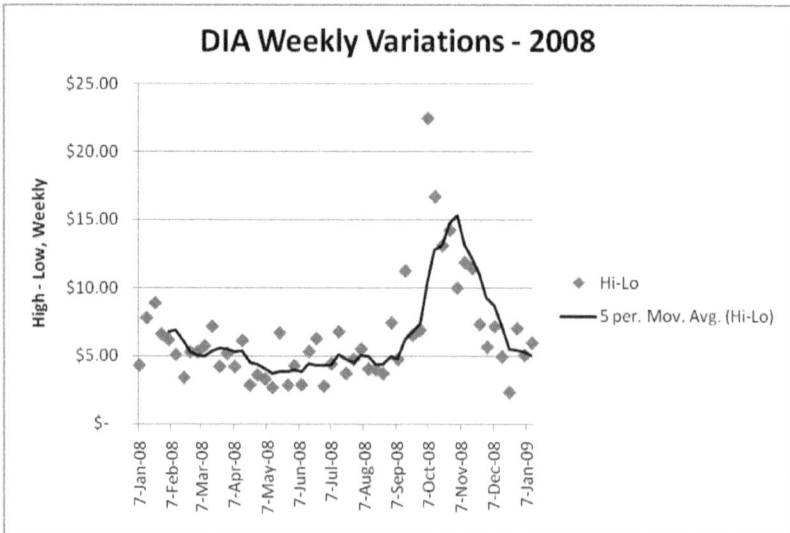

Here you can see clearly that you can certainly make at least one trade a week.

With the basic strategy of the $2 trading interval, one round trip makes you $200. Thus, if you do one round trip a week, you would make $10,400 a year.

If you do one round trip a day, with roughly 250 trading days a year, you would make $50,000 a year.

Therefore, if you followed this strategy, you may make somewhere between $10,000 and $50,000 a year. If you prepare $200,000 for this strategy, you may make somewhere between 5% and 25% per year. This is not a bad return.

Actually, you will also get some monthly dividends by owning DIA. These will add to your return when you follow this strategy. In 2008, it paid a dividend of about $2.60 per share, amounting to about 2~3%.

Therefore, owning DIA is a good investment in itself and it beats the low interest rates you get from money market funds.

Chapter 6

Why DIA?

DIA is one of the ETF's based on the general market indices. The following discussion describes why DIA was selected for this strategy.

When a market index grows at 6~7% per year, some of its underlying stocks grow faster than the average and others slower. Therefore, if you choose the right stocks, you will be able to beat the market, so to speak. But, choosing the right stocks is not an easy thing to do. Even the professionals fail to do so year in and year out. There are almost no professionally managed mutual funds that beat the market index all the time.

There are three major indices that keep track of the market in general, they are:

- Dow Jones Industrials Average,

- Standard and Poor 500 Index, and

- Nasdaq 100 Index

There are many other indices but most of them track some specific portions of the market. For long term investment, it is best to stay with the three major indices mentioned above.

Investment in these three major indices is made easy by the presence of Exchange Traded Funds (ETF).

There are three ETF's corresponding to the three major indices:

- DIA – Diamonds Trust Series I for tracking the Dow Jones Industrials Average

- SPY – SPDR Trust Series I for tracking the Standard & Poor 500 Index

- QQQQ – Power Shares Trust Series I for tracking the Nasdaq-100 Index

Why DIA? Because

1. its underlying DJIA is historically the longest running market index,

2. it tracks fewer companies, but they are the largest and, most probably, the best,

3. these companies represent a wide diversity of businesses, and,

4. if any of them fails, there is an automatic substitution.

These are discussed in detail next.

6.1   Longest History

A longer history means the performance of the market index is more reliable. The 30 companies that make up the DJIA have changed over time. Each time one of the companies in the DJIA goes bankrupt or merges with another company, the people who manage the DJIA find another company to take the place of the company that gets de-listed. Therefore, the historical data of the DJIA presented above is a representation of the wisdom of the people who select the companies in the DJIA, as well as a record of the performance of these companies in general.

The S&P 500 started in 1957 and thus its history is only slightly more than one half as long as that of the DJIA. The S&P 500 is an equally good market index to follow. However, since the DJIA has a history of more than 80 years, I would rather follow the DJIA than the S&P 500.

Nasdaq has an even shorter history. It started in 1971.

6.2   Fewer Companies

The DJIA includes only 30 companies, compared with 500 in the S&P 500 and 100 in QQQQ, the EFT for Nasdaq. There are two views on the number of companies in an index:

- The more companies you have, the better the representation of the market in general.

- The fewer companies you have, the better the companies included.

It is your decision how to look at this. I go for the latter. With a smaller number of companies, it is more likely that they are the cream of the cream.

6.3   Diversity

The 30 companies that make up the DJIA are a diversified group. At the beginning of 2009 they are:

Aerospace:	Boeing Co. United Technologies Corp.
Aluminum:	Alcoa Inc.
Automobiles:	General Motors Corp.
Banks:	Bank of America Corp. Citigroup Inc. JPMorgan Chase & Co.
Broadcasting & Entertainment:	Walt Disney Co.
Broadline Retailers:	Wal-Mart Stores Inc.
Commercial Vehicles & Trucks:	Caterpillar Inc.
Commodity Chemicals:	E.I. DuPont de Nemours & Co.
Computer Hardware:	Hewlett-Packard Co.
Computer Services:	International Business Machines Corp.
Consumer Finance:	American Express Co.

Diversified Industrials:	3M Co.
	General Electric Co.
Fixed Line Telecommunications:	AT&T Inc.
	Verizon Communications Inc.
Food Products:	Kraft Foods Inc. Co.
Home Improvement Retailers:	Home Depot Inc.
Integrated Oil & Gas:	Chevron Corp.
	Exxon Mobil Corp.
Nondurable Household Products:	Procter & Gamble Co.
Pharmaceuticals:	Johnson & Johnson
	Merck & Co. Inc.
	Pfizer Inc.
Restaurants & Bars:	McDonald's Corp.
Semiconductors:	Intel Corp.
Soft Drinks:	Coca-Cola Co.
Software:	Microsoft Corp.

Information source:
https://www.djaverages.com/?view=industrial&page=components

These are all big capital companies and they represent a great diversity in their businesses.

Diversity has been one of the important guidelines for investing and, as shown above, the DJIA provides it.

6.4   Automatic Substitution

The main attraction of investing in market indices is their safety.

Individual companies may come and go. Some may go bankrupt or disappear. Even the largest and best run companies may fail. When one of the companies in the DJIA fails, the committee that runs the DJIA replaces it with another good company they find. Thus, if you own DIA and if one of the companies in the DJIA fails, you do not have to do anything like liquidating the shares of the failed company from your portfolio. Instead, it will be automatically replaced by that committee.

For example, in the great market crash of 2008, American International Group (AIG), which was a component of the DJIA, became financially unsustainable by itself and needed to be rescued by the Treasury. On September 22, 2008, it was replaced by Kraft Foods.

If you own DIA on September 22, 2008, without you doing anything, the Dow Jones & Company, a subsidiary of News Corporation, the company responsible for maintaining the DJIA, replaced the weakened American International Group with the robust Kraft Foods.

How convenient! Dow Jones & Company screens out the losers for you and replaces them with winners without you asking for it or doing anything about it.

Suppose you own the stock of a failing company, you would have no recourse but to unload it at a fire-sale price and pay dearly for a healthier company of your choice.

Only two of the 30 companies on the original (1928) DJIA list are still on the list today.

They are:

- General Electric Company (GE), and

- General Motors Corporation (GMC)

By the end of 2008, in the midst of the market crash, even GMC was on the verge of bankruptcy and asking Congress for a last ditch financial rescue. Even GE has seen its share price plummeted at the beginning of 2009.

Since the Dow Jones 30 Industrial Average was established in 1928, most of the original 30 companies have disappeared from today's list while the DJIA has been marching upward all these years.

These companies have been taken off the list because they no longer are qualified to be on it, have disappeared (or gone bankrupt), or have merged into other companies.

Therefore, if you had invested in the individual companies in the original DJIA, you would have seen quite a few bankruptcies and mergers and would have had to readjust your portfolio just as the DJIA adjusted its components. On the other hand, if DIA had been available in 1928 and you had bought it at about $3 a share (the DJIA was equal to about 300) and if you still held it today, with its current value at around $90 a share, you would have gained almost 30 times, plus the dividends, without doing anything, thanks to the people who managed the DJIA all these years.

It is safe to say that the U.S. economy will keep growing and these market indices are here to stay and they may never go to zero, unless something catastrophic happens to the U.S. economy. With a healthy U. S. economy, the people who manage the DJIA will continue to maintain the DJIA with only the best companies in the U. S.

Chapter 7

Advantages of the Strategy

The strategy has many advantages, some of which are listed below:

- Market index

  DIA is based on a general market index, DJIA, and many advantages come with it, some of which are listed below.

- Long history

  The DJIA is the longest running general market index and thus it provides a greater dependability in interpreting its performance.

- Diversification

  The DJIA provides it

- No time pressure

Holding the long position at all times removes the time pressure for action.

- Dividend

  The companies constituting the DJIA mostly pay great dividends regularly

- Automatic replacement of failed companies

  As the DJIA readjusts its component companies, only the best companies are in the list. All the weakened or failed companies are weeded out from the list automatically.

- Catching both highs and lows

  The strategy buys as the market falls and sells as the market rises, and, thereby, it catches both the market highs and lows.

- Not making mistakes by being emotional

  The strategy follows rigid buy and sell guidelines, thereby removing the emotional component of trading which tends to get us into trouble.

Chapter 8

Limitations, Faith, and Risks

The strategy presented in this book has limitations.

- It only applies when the DJIA is below 10,000.

- If the DJIA goes considerably lower than 10,000, say, 5,000, you might consider whether or not you should continue with the strategy, suspend it, or liquidate the investment.

The history of the DJIA indicates the uncertainties and fickleness of the stock market and, therefore, the risks involved in investing in it.

You must be aware of these risks when you invest.

We do not know what is going to happen next in the market:

- No growth?

- Robust growth?

- Or, a retreat?

That the DJIA grew at an average of 6~7% per year is something that happened in the past.

But, what we really want to know is what we may expect from the market in the future. And, nobody can foresee the future exactly.

There is no guarantee that the past will repeat itself. But, sometimes, the past is a good indication of what is to come. The past is the only information we have and it may provide us with a glimpse into the future.

The stock market represents the wealth of the companies which are parts of it. The sales and profits of the companies may grow with the expanding market and rising prices. These factors, in turn, are affected by things such as improvement in productivity, population growth, and inflation, just to name a few.

There is a limit to how fast and how far these factors can grow.

Based on the past performance of the DJIA, we can say the following:

> Unless there will be some unforeseen drastic changes in the U. S. economy, the growth of the DJIA at an average rate of 6~7% may continue in the future.

The statement above is very important. It is the backbone of everything this book talks about here. We may plan our investment based on this expectation.

It is also very important to bear in mind that:

1. This expectation is based on past experience, and
2. There is no guarantee that the future is going to be the same as the past.

These two statements seem to be in contradiction.

But, actually they are not.

We can say that past experience is the only data we have on which to bet our future, since nobody can say for sure what future holds.

However, we can also say that in making our investments, we should always be on the lookout for situations that are not the same as those that happened in the past.

In other words, we cannot bet our future "blindly" on what had happened in the past.

Let me clarify once more.

Past behavior of the market is the only information we have that is certain. Therefore, a prediction of the future market movement based on its past behavior is the best we have.

But, don't you bet everything on it.

Have some reservations at all time.

Be cautious.

There will always be something unexpected.

And, nobody can tell you when the unexpected will happen, how it will happen and what it will be.

Remember:

- Risk is not avoidable.

- Be aware of the risk.

- Take steps to limit the risk.

In summary:

- Make a good analysis as best as you can of the patterns in the past performance of the market.

- Assume the future is an extension of the past.

- But be prepared for the unforeseen, as the future becomes present.

There may be some basic changes occurring now in the U.S., as well as around the world, that will cause the U. S. economy to grow at either a faster or a slower rate than it has in the past. We do not know what these changes are yet. As a result, future growth of the stock market may not repeat that of the past.

The flat growth of the stock market from 1960 to 1980 happened to coincide with the Vietnam War when we, the Americans, pursued a strategy of "both guns and butter" under the Johnson Administration.

That may be a pure coincidence.

However, the market recovered after the long stall between 1960 and 1980.

Now we have wars going on in the Middle East and our government is pumping huge sum of money into the economy to keep it going. We do not know whether all of these will lead to another long flat period for the stock market or whether something totally unexpected will happen.

If you follow the strategy laid out in this book at this troubled time, you do so with the faith that the U. S. economy will eventually right itself and will continue to grow at its historical rate.

Without such faith, you should not invest in the stock market now.

Even with such faith, you should always be on the watch for the effects of any of the current and future events that may change the future course of the market.

If, and when, any change in the market does occur, you will have to change the way you invest.

This book assumes that such changes are not going to happen.

This does not mean such changes will not happen.

When they do happen, it will be a whole new ball game, and you would be well advised to stop following this book.

Good Luck!

Glossary

Buy and hold is a long term investment strategy based on the concept that in the long run financial markets give a good rate of return despite periods of volatility or decline. From: http://en.wikipedia.org/wiki/Buy_and_hold

DIA is an ETF. Its full name is Dow Diamonds ETF. The objective of the Trust is to provide investment results that generally correspond to the price and yield performance of the Dow Jones Industrial Average. It is listed on the U.S. AMEX exchange. Its fund manager is State Street Global Markets, LLC. From: http://etf.stock-encyclopedia.com/DIA.html

The **Dow Jones Industrial Average**, also called the **DJIA**, is one of several stock market indices, created by nineteenth-century *Wall Street Journal* editor and Dow Jones & Company co-founder Charles Dow. It is an index that shows how certain stocks have traded. Dow compiled the index to gauge the performance of the industrial sector of the American stock market. It is the second-oldest U.S. market index, after the Dow Jones Transportation Average, which Dow also created. The average is computed from the stock prices of 30 of the largest and most widely held public companies in the United States. From: http://en.wikipedia.org/wiki/Dow_Jones_Industrial_Average

An **exchange-traded fund** (or **ETF**) is an investment vehicle traded on stock exchanges, much like stocks. An ETF holds assets such as stocks or bonds and trades at approximately the same price as the net asset value of its underlying assets over the course of the trading day. Most ETFs track an index, such as the Dow Jones Industrial Average or the S&P 500. From: http://en.wikipedia.org/wiki/Exchange-traded_fund

In investment, a **Good Till Cancelled (GTC)** order is an order to buy or sell a security which remains in effect until executed or canceled. In other words, a GTC order will continue indefinitely until the specified parameters are met, whilst a normal day order would cancel automatically after the market closes, requiring the investor to make a new order the next day if desired. From: http://en.wikipedia.org/wiki/Good_'Til_Cancelled

Historical trend line is a straight line drawn through the past prices of the Dow Jones Industrial Average in order to gauge the average progression of this market index. The extension of this line is used to guess at the future movement of the index.

A **lot** is a group of stocks that is bought or sold in a transaction.

Markup is the difference between the prices of a pair of buy and sell transactions.

Order book is a record of sell and buy orders waiting to be executed.

Position is the stock you buy and hold for a certain period of time.

Trading interval is the difference in the strike prices between the two consecutive buy orders.

Trading range is the range of the DJIA within which a particular investment strategy is applicable.

Trading size is the number of shares bought or sold on each transaction.

Index

www.ingramcontent.com/pod-product-compliance
Lightning Source LLC
Chambersburg PA
CBHW031952190326
41519CB00007B/776